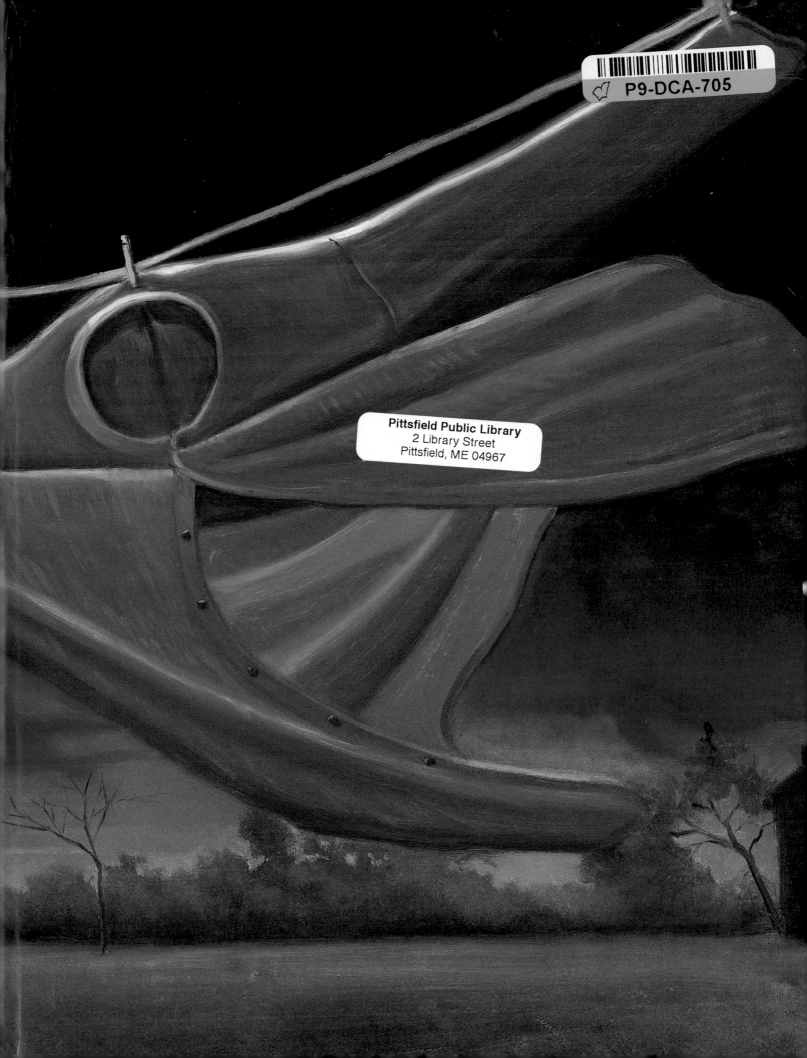

For Ashley
—Candice Ransom

To Deborah Williams-Velasquez for
her inspirational courage and strength
—Eric Velasquez

First published in the United States of America in 2003 by
Walker Publishing Company, Inc.

Published simultaneously in Canada by Fitzhenry and Whiteside, Markham, Ontario L3R 4T8

For information about permission to reproduce selections from
this book, write to Permissions, Walker & Company, 435 Hudson Street, New York, New York 10014

Library of Congress Cataloging-in-Publication Data

Ransom, Candice F., 1952-
Liberty Street / Candice Ransom ; illustrations by Eric Velasquez.— [1st U.S. ed.]
p. cm.
Summary: Young Kezia is a slave, living in nineteenth-century Fredericksburg, Virginia, until her mother helps her escape. Includes historical notes.
ISBN 0-8027-8869-6 — ISBN 0-8027-8871-8 (re)
[1. Slavery—Fiction. 2. African Americans—Fiction. 3. Underground railroad—Fiction. 4. Fredericksburg (Va.)—History—19th century—Fiction.] I.
Velasquez, Eric, ill. II. Title.

PZ7.R1743Li 2003
[E]—dc21
2002041481

The artist used oil on Fabriano paper to create the illustrations for this book.

Book design by Marva J. Martin

Visit Walker & Company's Web site at www.walkeryoungreaders.com

Printed in Hong Kong

2 4 6 8 10 9 7 5 3 1

LIBERTY STREET

Candice Ransom

Illustrations by Eric Velasquez

Walker & Company
New York

I was born on wash day.

"Did you have to work that day?" I once asked Mama.

"Our people work every day, Kezia," she said.

Old Zeus, Mama, and me, the three of us belong
to Missus Grace, a widow lady. We work for her,
candlelight to candlelight, day in and day out.

Monday is always wash day.

Tuesday is ironing day.

Wednesday is market day.

Thursday Mama sews and I mend.

On Friday Mama cleans Missus Grace's house while I polish the brass and silver.

Saturdays Mama weeds the garden. I help Zeus groom the carriage horses.

But Sunday! Sweet Sunday!

We get liberty. After Mama cooks Missus Grace's dinner, we have the afternoon off to go visiting without passes. Mama and I take the dirt path downtown. White folks own the streets like they own us. But this path is ours, worn by the pounding of many bare feet.

We call it Liberty Street.

Used to be folks came to see us on Sundays. They'd eat Mama's peach pies and listen to Papa's stories. When folks started to leave, Papa would say, "Don't go yet. Long time between now and mornin'." People couldn't stay—the constables would catch them. But they laughed at Papa's joke.

Then Missus Grace sold Papa to pay her husband's debts. The dark seemed darker without him. Mama sat by my bed and rocked me in her arms.

"Inside your fear is a kernel of strength," she said. "Look deep and you'll find it."

She told me she'd heard of a new secret school.

"Can I go?" I ask Mama.

Missus Grace spells words in front of us when she speaks to other white folks. I want to know what those words are.

The next Sunday, Mama sends me to Miss Eulalie, a free lady who will be our teacher.

"Watch out for the constable," she warns.

It's against the law for Miss Eulalie to teach and for us to learn. White folks are afraid we might write our own passes. If we are caught, we could get thirty-nine lashes.

At Miss Eulalie's house, I look at her dishes and pictures and books. So many books! We meet in a back room with a low door and no windows. Miss Eulalie begins our first lesson, the letters of the alphabet. I can't wait to make words.

I recite the ABCs while Mama rubs on her board. I spell new words as I spread Missus Grace's hankies on the grass to dry. I write my name in the sky.

KEZIA

Mama bends over the ironing board.

"How come you're ironing? It's not Tuesday," I say.

"From now on," she declares, "I do washin' every day. Missus Grace is bondin' you out to her sister in Richmond. You could be gone for years. I'm workin' extra to buy your freedom."

Take me away from Mama? That can't happen!

One Sunday, Miss Eulalie tells us about Canada, a place where all of our people are free. It is cold and snowy there. Then we hear the constable's shoes clump on the cobblestones. He stops outside our door. We all fall still until he moves on.

That night I dream of that Canada-place, where every day is liberty. I dream of being a teacher like Miss Eulalie.

The next day, Mama pulls a white shirt out of the clothes basket.

"It's supposed to rain," I say.

"I know," she says. She hangs the shirt on the line anyway.

Mama counts her savings. Silver coins slip through her fingers like a glimpse of freedom.

"Not enough," she says sadly. "Missus Grace is sendin' you away next week."

I do not want to leave home. I do not want to leave school.

Sunday night it is my turn to read when there comes a bang at Miss Eulalie's house door.

"*Shhh!*" She closes the door to the windowless room, then drags something heavy across the door to hide it. We quickly douse the lights. It is as dark as a crow's pocket in there. My stomach becomes a hard knot of fear.

We hear Miss Eulalie open the front door.

"Evenin'," she says, smooth as butter.

"What's going on here?" the constable demands. "I heard voices."

"I live alone," Miss Eulalie says. "You must have heard me talking to my cat."

"What cat?" asks the constable.

"Oh, he hides when strangers are here," says Miss Eulalie.

"I'll just look around," says the constable.

We hear his boots thump throughout the house. The boots pause near the room we are hiding in. None of us breathe. I spell "Canada" silently to keep my heart quiet. At last he turns away.

When the constable is gone,
Miss Eulalie lets us out. I am crying.   The others
go home, but I stay, and Miss Eulalie shows me a picture of Canada. All
that bright snow chases away the dark.

 "I heard tell of a tunnel that leads to the river," she says. "Once across,
a body would be on her way to Canada."

Turns out, Mama knows about the tunnel, too.

"Tonight you will walk under the white folks' streets and not be seen," she says.

"What about you?" I ask.

"My time will come later," she says. "There is only room for one more in the boat." Mama plucks a red shirt from the basket. Then she packs biscuits in a sack and stitches silver and a note from Miss Eulalie into my apron. The note is for the people I will live with in Canada. Mama moves briskly, but her face is sad.

"I don't want to go without you," I say.

"You can go to school there," Mama says.

"I'm scared," I tell her.

"You'll be fine," Mama says. "Remember, look inside for your strength." She holds me tight, then lets me go.

Zeus is waiting at our back door to guide me through the shadowy streets.

We hide in the bushes whenever we hear footsteps. Then he rushes me into a house.

Miss Eulalie is there with the others.
"Are you coming, too?" I whisper.
"No. I must stay here to help
our people run." She unlatches a
trapdoor in the floor. A flight of
stairs disappears into blackness.
It is darker than a grave down
there. I freeze in place.
"Kezia!" urges Miss Eulalie.

If I don't move, we will miss the boat. But if I move, the darkness will swallow me. Then I remember my mother's words. Inside my fear of the dark is the light of freedom! All I have to do is walk toward it. I stumble on moss-slick bricks. My feet carry me down. At the bottom someone lights a lantern. I gasp in the stale air. We walk under the town, right under the white folks' houses. We tumble out of an old warehouse by a river. A boat is waiting for us.

I look back at the town and wonder how Miss Eulalie fixed our escape. She couldn't do it alone. And then I know . . . My mother! Rubbing clothes on her board, stirring with her trouble stick, my mother is invisible. She found out about the tunnel, the street to freedom. She figured when it was safe to run. The red shirt told everyone to leave that night. She stayed behind to help others, risking punishment if she is caught.

The boat rocks as steadily as my mother's strong arms.
I will get to that cold and snowy Canada-land. I will work hard
in school and become a teacher. And I will send for my mother.
After all, it's a long time between now and morning.

AUTHOR'S NOTE

People often think of slaves as having worked on big plantations. Slaves worked in smaller households in towns and cities, as well.

I have set my story in pre–Civil War Fredericksburg, Virginia. Under the steep city streets are tunnels dating back to pre–Revolutionary War days. The tunnels may have been used for transporting tobacco to ships.

Free blacks were not allowed to educate their children, and it was against the law to teach slave children. Secret schools were held in basements and parlors. Teachers risked arrest to teach children to read.

It was a common practice to "bond out" slaves. For example, a slave owner might "rent" his blacksmith to a neighboring plantation or his young housemaid to another owner for a period of time.

The "clothesline telegraph" was a code used during the Civil War, when many slaves escaped to freedom. A white shirt signaled it was not safe to run. A red shirt meant "Go!"

Liberty Street really exists in Fredericksburg. It is a paved street based on the path followed by slaves who were "at liberty." In pre–Civil War days, that path was called Free Alley and led downtown. Free Alley is still a footpath, now used as a shortcut across town.